SUPERBASE 11

UPPER HEYFORD

SUPERBASE 11

UPPER HEYFORD

Aardvarks and Ravens

Published in 1990 by Osprey Publishing
Limited

59 Grosvenor Street, London W1X 9DA

British Library Cataloguing in Publication Data

Davison, Jon
    Upper Heyford. — (Superbase)
    1. Great Britain. American air bases
    I. Title   II. Series
    358.4′17′0941

ISBN 0 85045 913 3

Editor Tony Holmes
Page design by Paul Kime
Printed in Hong Kong

Front cover An F-111E waits for the word inside its bomb-proof shelter, wings swept fully back at 72.5 degrees in order to maximize the amount of space available for servicing and arming requirements.

Title pages If war ever came, Heyford's F-111Es would be expected to step on the loud pedal and launch against high-value targets such as airfields located deep in enemy territory. Initial attacks would almost certainly be carried out using conventional munitions, but the F-111E is also equipped to carry B-61 tactical nuclear weapons

Back cover A general view of an Aardvark parked in the open. Most USAF tailcodes correspond to the aircraft's parent base, although 'UH' is difficult to discern in these days of low-visibility markings

Opposite Bathed in sunlight outside its protective hangar, this F-111E exudes Mach 2-plus performance. The long, elegant nose of the F-111 earned it the endearing nickname of 'Aardvark'—in reality a rather ponderous South American anteater

Introduction

Royal Air Force Upper Heyford takes its name from the nearby quintessential English village in the heart of rural Oxfordshire. The airfield dates back to World War I and has long been associated with bomber aircraft; it is probably the only airbase in the world to have had a bomber named after it (the Handley Page H.P.50 Heyford, which first flew in June 1930).

During and immediately after World War II, the base was used by Operational Training Units of Bomber Command operating Wellingtons, and later Mosquitoes and Oxfords. Upper Heyford was briefly home to a Dakota-equipped parachute training school before it became one of several RAF airfields to be occupied by USAF Strategic Air Command. The base was under SAC control from June 1953 until March 1965, during which time the windows of local houses were well and truly rattled by the comings and goings of Convair B-36s, Boeing KB-29P tankers and Boeing B-47s. Strategic reconnaissance versions of the B-36 and B-47 bombers were also deployed there. The first Tactical Air Command unit to be based at Upper Heyford was the 66th Tactical Reconnaissance Wing, whose RF-101C Voodoos had redeployed there from Laon in France. The F-111E strike/bombers (interdictors in European parlance) of the 20th Tactical Fighter Wing have been residents since June 1970, the EF-111A Raven tactical electronic warfare aircraft of the 42nd Electronic Combat Squadron following in 1983.

This Superbase book is dedicated to all the personnel who fly and maintain both models of the General Dynamics F-111 at RAF Upper Heyford. Special thanks are due to Captain Alvina Mitchell, M/Sgt Bill Thornton, Sgt Kevin Koelling and Richard Colley of the 20th TFW's Public Affairs Office; F-111 drivers Captains Derek Jones and Ken Williams of the 77th TFS; and Captains Dave Wente and Chris Glaze of the 42nd ECS.

A native of New Zealand, Jon Davison is a professional freelance photographer who is currently based in Oxford. He enjoys taking risks to capture that elusive image. His published work includes *Oxford Inspired Images 1* and *2*, *Cambridge* and *Mexico's Yucatan Peninsula*. His trusty Hassleblad and Nikon F3 performed impeccably despite sub-zero temperatures inside an open, unheated concrete aircraft shelter in the middle of winter. On one occasion it was so cold that his fingers stuck to the camera body. The film used was exclusively Fujichrome 100 and 400 ISO on 35 mm and 6 × 6 cm formats. Lenses ranged from 16 mm fisheye to 1200 mm telephoto.

A self-portrait of your intrepid photographer perched on the rear fuselage of an F-111E. The missing panels on this machine bear mute testimony to the complex maintenance required to keep the big swinger in the air

Contents

Aardvark

Carrying a pair of 600 US gallon fuel tanks under its pivotable wing pylons, 68-067 'lets it all hang out' as it prepares to touch down at RAF Upper Heyford

Right Spot the difference: an EF-111A 'Spark Vark' electronic warfare aircraft is number one to land as it breaks away from its partner, an F-111E

Above Characteristic stabilizer droop indicates that the aircraft's hydraulic system is okay. In the event of total hydraulic failure in flight, the horizontal stabilizer would rapidly reach either full up or full down deflection, with disastrous consequences

Top Canopies cracked open and aircrew ladders attached, an F-111E stands ready for an early morning mission. Although 'Aardvark' has become its popular nickname, the F-111 is often referred to as the 'Lizard' at Upper Heyford

Touch and go. After a rock steady approach and brisk short finals, this F-111E burnt rubber for a few seconds until the pilot hit the 'burners to send his mount back into the firmament

Above Trailing undesirable wing tip vortices (which could give away the presence of the aircraft to a sharp-eyed fighter pilot, and tell him that his quarry is manoeuvring hard), an Aardvark flicks into a turn over the Oxfordshire countryside. If the crew detects an enemy fighter coming at them early enough they can use the aircraft's power and swing-wing capability to outrun their opponent, who would soon run low on fuel if he tried to pursue them. But at night or in bad weather, a low flying F-111 would be almost invulnerable to air attack (*Sgt David S Nolan, USAFE*)

Right An Aardvark sniffs the morning air from within the confines of its hangar. The 20th Tactical Fighter Wing, 3rd Air Force, has been resident at Upper Heyford since 1970 and is equipped with three Tactical Fighter Squadrons of F-111Es: the 55th TFS (blue fin stripe), 77th TFS (red fin stripe) and the 79th TFS (yellow 'tiger' fin stripe)

Overleaf Like all front-line combat aircraft, the F-111 is very expensive to operate, only more so. To save Uncle Sam valuable dollars, the flight simulator is utilized as much as possible

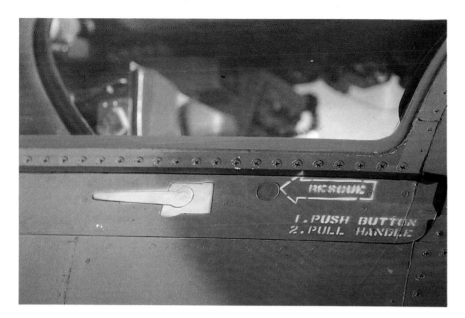

The red paint which surrounds this Aardvark's canopy indicates that the panels have been replaced by a new, flexible, multi-layer material capable of surviving severe bird strikes. The material is actually designed to buckle on impact; in extreme cases the 'foreign object' can end up inside the cockpit, while the canopy pops back into its original shape

Left From head-on, the Aardvark belies its namesake's long nose and looks almost like a bird of prey. The bulk of this 50-ton machine is readily apparent

Above Equipped with attack and terrain-following radars, inertial navigation and numerous 'black boxes', the F-111 was the world's first genuine all-weather strike/bomber aircraft. '*We have systems in this aircraft that people wouldn't believe. I'd say that during a typical mission we would use only a quarter of its potential; this aircraft was 20 years ahead of its time, without a doubt,*' says an enthusiastic F-111 pilot. As it penetrates to the target, carefully avoiding the known air defence radars and SAM sites already programmed into its nav/attack system, the F-111 is sneaky, elusive and fast. The TFR system allows the aircraft to be flown automatically as low as 200 feet above ground level at speeds in excess of Mach One

After flexing its spoilers, 68-047 'lights the pipes' for take-off. Unless there is a major breakthrough in arms control negotiations between NATO and the Warsaw Pact, the sun is unlikely to set on F-111 operations from RAF Upper Heyford before the year 2000. Due to the cost escalation which affected all F-111 production the USAF took delivery of a mere 94 E-models, but these have proved sufficient to maintain a strike force of 72 aircraft with the 20th TFW at Upper Heyford. Four squadrons of the more advanced F-111F (digital avionics and more powerful engines) equip the 48th TFW at RAF Lakenheath in Suffolk

Above Rivalled, but arguably unsurpassed by the Panavia Tornado and F-15E Strike Eagle, the F-111s at Upper Heyford and Lakenheath provide NATO with a flexible, all-weather, round-the-clock strike capability. Aardvark 031 of the 77th TFS gets a tow as the base shivers in temperatures of minus 15 degrees Celsius

Right Good Morning Upper Heyford. Carbon arc lights illuminate an Aardvark waiting to launch the first mission of the day. Rebuilt when the F-111 came on the scene, Upper Heyford's substantial hangars (each blast door weighs a hefty five tons) are designed to withstand anything short of a direct nuclear detonation

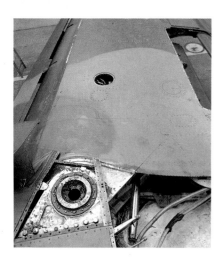

Above As any aircraft designer will tell you, 'the wing's the thing'. The pivot mechanism enables the F-111 to obtain the optimum sweep angle for take-off and landing, cruising, manoeuvring and low-level, high-speed penetration. Like the MiG-23/27, Tornado and B-1B, wing sweep position is selected manually by the pilot. Flap and slat areas are sprayed with highly visible red paint

Right and overleaf Back to the future. It's hard to imagine that this futuristic form first flew from General Dynamics' Fort Worth plant on 21 December 1964. A whole generation has grown up unaware of the political scandal surrounding the F-111's formative years, so here's a recap.

In 1960 the USAF created its Tactical Fighter Experimental (TFX) concept for a new weapons system to replace most of its 'Century Series' fighters. TFX would feature 'multi-role' afterburning turbofans, advanced navigation and weapon-aiming sub-systems, rough-field operating capability, a variable geometry wing incorporating high-lift slats and flaps, extensive use of titanium structure and the possibility of a crew escape capsule. Meanwhile, the Navy was looking for a new Fleet Defence Fighter to replace the cancelled XF6D Missileer and supersede the F-4 Phantom II, F-6

Skyray and F-8 Crusader. Enter the newly appointed Secretary for Defense, Robert S McNamara and his Washington 'whizz kids'.

McNamara was convinced that TFX could be developed to meet both Navy and Air Force requirements, saving hundreds of millions of dollars. 'Commonality' became both a buzzword and a sacred cow inside the Department of Defense. Thanks to its greater commonality, GD's design beat what many observers believed was a more realistic alternative proposal from Boeing–Wichita. Against the advice of service chiefs, McNamara authorized work to begin on the F-111A for the Air Force and F-111B for the Navy. This decision was politically unpopular, but the outcry was nothing compared to that which greeted the results of early test flights. First flown on 21 December 1964, the F-111A was branded a 'can of worms' by a chorus of critics: it was overweight, suffered from excessive aerodynamic drag, the temperamental TF30 turbofans were affected by faulty intake design and the swing wings did not work properly.

The Navy's F-111B fighter, developed in partnership with Grumman, was so obese and complex that the programme disintegrated in 1968. The F-111B's powerful Hughes AWG-9 fire-control radar, long-range Phoenix missiles and troublesome TF30s were inherited by its successor, the F-14 Tomcat. The F-111A survived and mostly overcame persistent technical problems to emerge as a combat proven strike/bomber aircraft. Compared to the initial F-111A (141 built), the E-model featured more efficient *Triple Plow II* jet inlets and ducts, which improved engine performance, and significantly reduced drag. It entered service with Tactical Air Command in October 1969

Above The vagaries of the English weather, especially its 'funny' cloud formations, leave a lasting impression on the new guys. I took this shot of a resting Aardvark just as the sun managed to find a gap in the overcast

Right The aircrews at Upper Heyford are a close knit bunch, and are rarely happier than when they can get airborne. Nevertheless, both the pilot and his Weapons Systems Officer (WSO) are required to rest for 12 hours before each mission. The F-111 is such a honey to fly that pilots transition onto type straight from the T-38 Talon advanced jet trainer—the difficult bit is learning how to handle an Aardvark under combat conditions as it hugs the terrain

Right Showtime! Shades of the USAF's Air Demonstration Squadron, the 'Thunderbirds', as a flight of F-111Es dip their wings in salute

Below Detail view of the in-flight refuelling receptacle fitted to the F-111, the target area for the nozzle of the refuelling boom carried by a KC-135 or KC-10 tanker aircraft

Overleaf An Aardvark gains altitude after take-off as a tractor and gang mower help to keep the airfield's lush greenery in check. The 'Vark is no slouch and soon reaches 300 knots as it climbs away

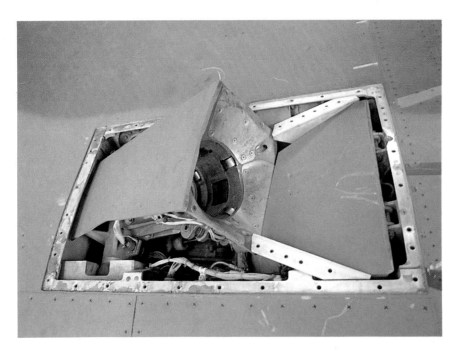

Preceding pages Blast off. With 'burners glowing white hot, an Aardvark heads into the golden afterglow

These pages Photographing an F-111 on short finals is not recommended, as the noise is truly ear-splitting. Standing near the end of the runway, one can hear the air 'shredding' overhead, followed by the noise of the wingtip vortices as they race and swirl; altogether an eerie, whistling snapping sound. **Above** Just visible aft of the main gears is the Westinghouse ALQ-119(V) tactical jamming pod, unique to aircraft deployed in the USAFE theatre. Internal chaff and flare dispensers are also carried. The wings are set fully forward (sweep angle 16 degrees) to minimize approach speed

Overleaf A pair of Aardvarks in formation low over the Oxfordshire landscape, laden with a dozen Mk 82 Snakeye bombs apiece. The leading aircraft is from the 55th TFS, its partner from the 79th TFS; both carry their 6000 pound bomb loads on multiple ejector racks (MERs). To keep stores aligned with the airstream the four inner pylons rotate as the wings are swept; four outer non-swivelling pylons may be added, but these have to be jettisoned if the wings are swept beyond 26 degrees. All stores are carried externally as the internal weapons bay can also be occupied by additional fuel tankage

Ravens

Left An EF-111A Raven of the 42nd Electronic Combat Squadron awaits its crew. The 42nd ECS is administered by the 66th Tactical Reconnaissance Wing, 17th Air Force at Sembach Air Base in West Germany, but the squadron's aircraft operate from Upper Heyford

Above Home to roost. A Raven flares out for landing as the day's flying comes to an end

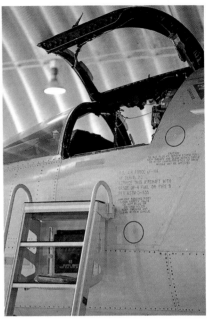

Produced by Grumman, the EF-111A tactical electronic warfare aircraft is an extensively reworked version of the original F-111A bomber. Although much of the airframe has been modified to accommodate a comprehensive range of jamming and sensing equipment, the expensive tweaks applied to the TF30 powerplant have allowed the old *Triple Plow I* jet intake arrangement (identified by the drag-inducing plate in front of the inlet), to be retained. A total of 42 airframes have been converted into EF-111As

Left Located in an unmistakable fairing atop the vertical stabilizer are no fewer than 18 radar receivers associated with the Raven's Raytheon AN/ALQ-99E jamming system, which is specially adapted from the equipment carried by the US Navy's EA-6B Prowlers. The fuel vent mast or 'dumper' is located at the bottom of the blunt tail section. Many antipodean airshow crowds, as well as those in the UK, have vivid memories of the spectacular 'torching' displays given by F-111s of the Royal Australian Air Force. (The RAAF ordered 24 C-models in 1967, the same year that Britain cancelled its requirement for 50 F-111Ks; the Aussie Aardvarks were finally delivered in 1973). Torching involves igniting dumped fuel with the afterburners, producing a 100-foot flame, the heat from which can be felt on the faces of spectators. More seriously, torching can be used in a desperate attempt to throw off infra-red guided missiles if other countermeasures fail

Above Designed with rough-field and carrier operations in mind, the unusual main landing gear arrangement of the F-111 is very reassuring for the pilot. Because both main gears form a single unit, a 'one-up, one-down' situation never occurs. However, the narrow track can make life a little uncomfortable for the pilot in severe crosswinds

These pages and top right overleaf Captain Dave Wente (pilot) and Electronic
Warfare Officer (EWO) Captain Chris Glaze (on the right in both pictures),
prepare for a hop over the Scottish Highlands. Their grey ID patches indicate an
'Electric Fox' or 'Spark Vark' flight crew. Meticulous planning begins days
before take-off to ensure that the Raven (the aircraft's more prosaic, official
name), is where it needs to be at the right time during all phases of the mission.
Crews are constantly refining their operational techniques in order to operate
the aircraft just that little bit more effectively every time they launch. As one
pilot put it: '*If you're not flying, you're studying. And if you're not studying,
you're getting behind . . .*' After donning G-suits and picking up their personal
kit, our intrepid aeronauts are ready to board the 'van' (see overleaf)

Left and above Captain Chris Glaze takes the EWO's right-hand seat and pulls on his HGU-55/P lightweight helmet as Captain Dave Wente settles in before commencing the pre-start checks. The cockpit-cum-escape module is pressurized and air conditioned, allowing the crew to operate unencumbered by pressure suits or umbilical personal equipment connectors

Left A view of the Raven's cockpit, revealing the two all-important yellow escape module ejection handles between the seats, and the single yellow handle on the canopy centre beam which deploys the three parachutes. After explosive separation from the aircraft, the module is propelled about 300 feet in order to clear any debris and/or allow enough time for the parachutes to deploy if it all goes pear-shaped near the ground. If the crew come down on *terra firma*, the module doubles as a ready-made shelter and if they splash down in the ocean, it doubles as a boat to keep them afloat until help arrives. Believe it or not, if the sea is rough the pilot's control stick is used as a bilge pump handle. One of the few shortcomings of this 'luxury' survival system is that it does not possess the zero-speed, zero-altitude ('zero–zero') capability of the current generation of ejection seats. The small yellow handle on the far left of the instrument panel, intended to release an arrestor hook, is a legacy from the cancelled Navy F-111B fighter

Above Straps and lifelines secured, the Raven is ready to spool up

Right Raven 67-035 follows an F-111E along the taxiway after a mission involving 24 aircraft from the base. This angle accentuates the small amount of clearance between the main gear tyres and the fuselage. Sharp eyes will spot the open blow-in doors on the intake

Above and overleaf In common with their bomber colleagues, Raven crews cannot afford to be 'fair weather flyers'—they are expected to do their stuff come rain or shine, day or night. The 'Spark Vark' is equipped to perform three basic missions: the **barrier, or standoff mission**, in which the Raven operates in friendly airspace to mask the activities of NATO air assets from prying enemy radars (four or five Ravens would be capable of sustaining an electronic barrier from the Baltic to the Adriatic along the NATO front line); the **penetration, or escort mission**, in which the Raven would accompany strike packages deep into enemy territory; and the **close air support mission**, in which the Raven would protect 'mud-movers' operating in concert with NATO ground forces at the forward-edge of the battle area (FEBA). Despite all its electronic wizardry, the Raven cannot jam everything: the crew must be alert to the danger of being hit by infantry fire or optically-guided surface-to-air missiles

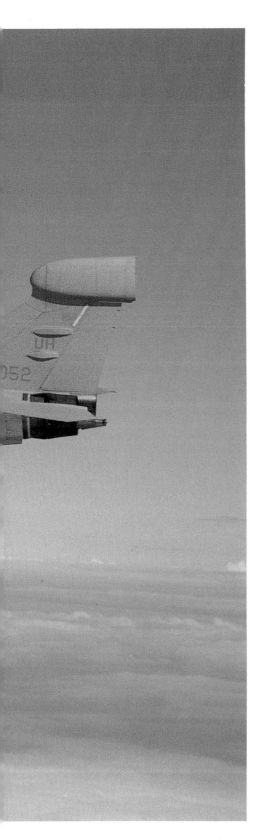

The airframe modifications required by the installation of the AN/ALQ-99E system have arguably given the Raven a more elegant and purposeful appearance than its A-model forebear, and possibly all the other members of family. The long canoe fairing under the forward fuselage houses an array of jamming transmitters (*Sgt David S Nolan, USAFE*)

Wings set fully forward, a Raven
cruises in its element. To operate the
entire electronic warfare system,
especially the jammers, the aircraft
has one million watts on tap—enough
power, it is claimed, to confound any
known radar or microwave 5000
turkeys in about 10 seconds! The
42nd Electronic Combat Squadron is
one of only two Raven units, the other
being the 390th ECS, 366th ECW,
based at Mountain Home AFB in Idaho
(*Sgt David S Nolan, USAFE*)

After yet another 'battle of the
beams', a Raven slips back into
Upper Heyford. The EWO controls
the tactical jamming and deception
activity by using an advanced CRT
digital display indicator and various
threat analysers

Above and top The F-111's variable geometry wing and its exceptional high-lift devices (slotted flaps and leading-edge slats extend along almost the entire span), mean that usually most of Heyford's 10,000 foot runway will not be required. Crabbing slightly into wind, this Raven will kiss the concrete at 140 knots and turn off the runway after a 2000-foot ground roll

Right Viewed from beyond the perimeter fence, a Raven and an Aardvark prepare to move out; spoilers are raised, slats and flaps extended and engines idling at 55% power

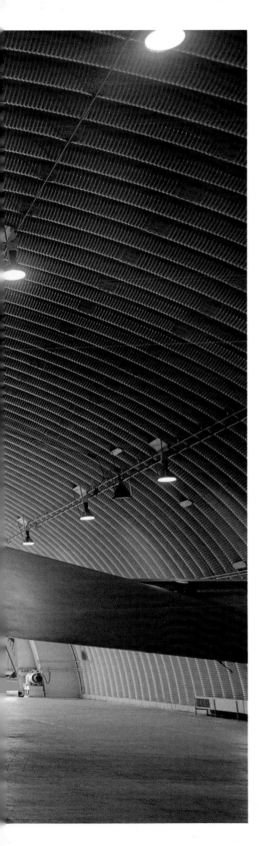

Raven haven: drip trays, wheel chocks and the mobile environmental control unit which provides cooling air to the avionics are all present in this perfect rear view. The close proximity of the engines minimizes asymmetric thrust problems, especially if an afterburner is lost on take-off. Four small fairings attached to the vertical stabilizer contain additional radar warning receivers

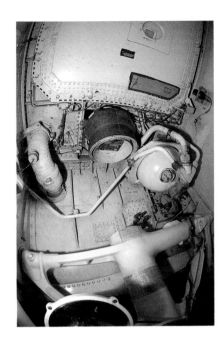

Above The nose gear well looking
aft; the rust-coloured circular object
in the middle of the picture is the
rocket motor nozzle which powers
the crew escape module. The top of
the nose gear vertical strut is
indicated by the bright yellow
warning placard

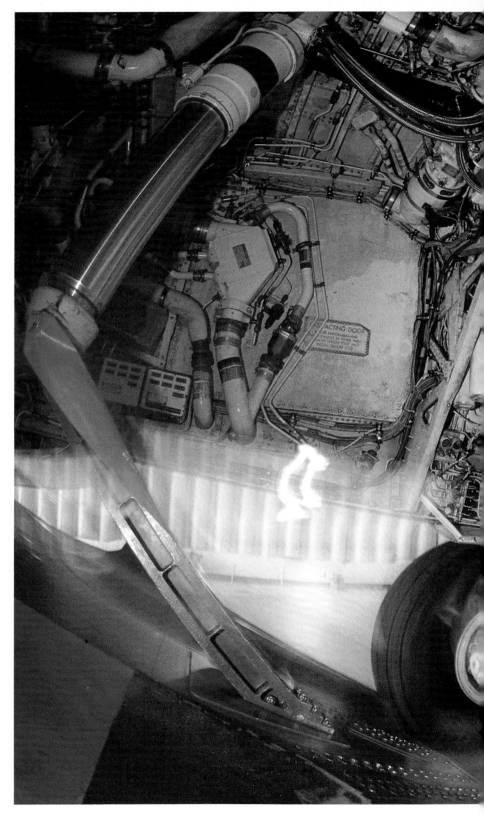

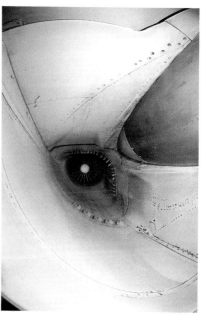

Left The main gear well looking aft; the big flat red item on the left is the gear door/speed brake. Due to their relatively low pressure and deep tread, the main gear tyres are good for 100 missions

Above A bird's-eye view down the starboard jet inlet of the EF-111A; note the complex arrangement of vortex generators on the duct

Below A Raven raises a quizzical 'eyebrow' for the benefit of the camera. The two little teardrop radomes mounted above the wing gloves house receivers for the ALQ-137 and ALR-62 radar warning systems. Plugged in just above the nose gear door is the external communications cable

Right Not the latest American cruise missile, but an unusual view of the Raven's electronic beak

This page Close-up of the port wing glove and ALR-62/ALQ-137 RWR

Overleaf Holy Spark Vark! Looking more like the 'Batmobile', this imposing study of the Raven emphasizes the ejector exhausts of the TF30 turbofans

The Workshop

Left Peeled ready for a regular preventative check-up, this Aardvark reveals its General Electric APQ-113 attack radar and the two 'eyes' of its Texas Instruments APQ-110 terrain-following radar (TFR). The TFR system was, and is, a remarkable example of sensor technology. After the pilot has selected the height above ground level at which he wants the aircraft to fly (preferably below 200 feet AGL to stay under the enemy radar horizon and to minimize the risk of 'snap-down' missile attacks from patrolling fighters), and decided from a choice of smooth, medium or hard ride settings, the TFR system takes over. In the event of a TFR failure the aircraft is automatically commanded into a 3G climb

Below The camouflage scheme applied to the F-111E is of Vietnam vintage, despite the fact that the USAF has only deployed the original A-model in South-east Asia. Taking appropriate precautions, a painter completes a spraying assignment

Left and top Two views of the Phase Maintenance shop taken from opposite ends of the facility. This is where the 20th Component Repair Squadron conduct their periodic inspections of all the F-111s based at Upper Heyford

Above Close-up of the trailing-edge flaps and flap tracks (try saying that fast); the flaps are at their fully extended 35-degree setting

Raven 66-030 being 'Phased'; airframe access is generally excellent, although many of the maintenance tasks are difficult and fiddly once you get the wraps off. All Ravens are painted in the low-visibility 'Grey Ghost' camouflage scheme

Left When you're checking a TF30's hydraulic lines it's okay to sit down on the job, as demonstrated by this female technician. The majority of powerplant inspection and maintenance tasks can be undertaken without having to separate the engines from the airframe

Above Most of the wing root shown here would serve to stabilize the escape module in both freefall and as it descends by parachute if the crew were forced to abandon ship. The explosive cutting chord shears the cockpit module from the fuselage along the break-line just visible between the canopy and the squadron emblem. An air bag inflates underneath the module to help cushion the landing. The module is a self-contained, independent vehicle within the aircraft, and is treated accordingly

This page The vast majority of the airframe inspection procedures applied to the Raven are identical to those required by the F-111E

Opposite and overleaf The 20th CRS Test Cell is where the TF30 turbofans are put through their paces. Thousands of gallons of water are pumped into the circular emission collector to reduce noise and prevent the chamber from overheating; engines are often run for many hours to enable accurate diagnostic and performance checks to be made. It is not too difficult to tell when engine testing is in progress as clouds of steam rise hundreds of feet over the facility. Air is drawn into the chamber through baffles in the roof, and the face of the engine is covered with a fine mesh screen (see inset overleaf)

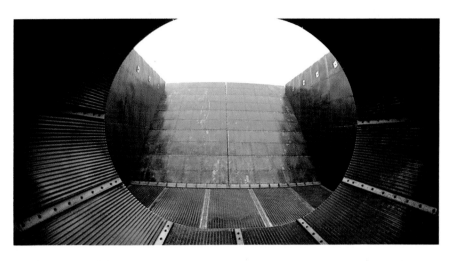

The 20th CRS also have hush houses where the whole aircraft can be accommodated

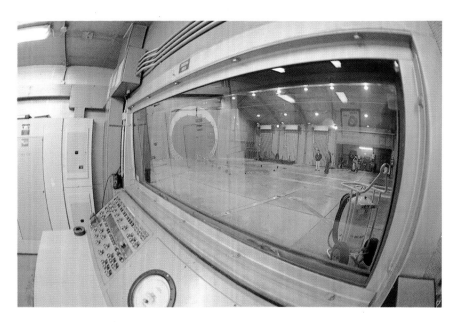

Above All of the action inside the engine test cell is monitored from behind the safety of thick glass in the control room. If an engine should catch fire and the cell is endangered, halon is pumped into the complex to purge the oxygen required for continued combustion

Right The Jet Propulsion Branch of the 20th CRS is responsible for the repair and servicing of the Pratt & Whitney TF30-P-3 engines fitted to the F-111E and EF-111A. A low by-pass ratio turbofan, the TF30 is able to deliver the high specific thrust and low specific fuel consumption performance which the F-111 requires to cruise for long periods at very low level. Measuring over 20 feet with afterburner, the engine has 16 compressor stages and delivers a thrust-to-weight ratio in dry power of 2.8:1. The output of the P-3 is modest compared to later versions, delivering 10,750 pounds of thrust dry and 18,500 pounds with afterburner; corresponding figures for the TF30-P-100 in the F-111F are 14,650/25,100

Left Compared to a conventional turbojet, the lower average exhaust velocity of a low by-pass ratio turbofan provides highly efficient dry-power cruise performance combined with tremendous afterburning thrust for take-off, low level acceleration and high level supersonic dash requirements. Although a turbofan is thirstier than a turbojet when afterburner is engaged, the penalty is acceptable because such high thrust levels are only required for short periods. This view of the business end of a TF30 reminds us that it was the world's first turbofan to be fitted with an afterburner. The basic concept of the TF30 has been copied by every other powerplant developed for today's front-line combat aircraft, and the knowledge gained by Pratt & Whitney as they strove to solve the engine's numerous problems was used to good effect in the development of the F100 turbofan for the F-15 Eagle and the F-16 Fighting Falcon

Above Airman 1st Class Brown begins the inspection of a newly-arrived TF30

Left Penetrator. The old analogue avionics fitted to the E-model are being replaced with digital equivalents as part of the $1.1 billion modification programme to update the attack/TFR radars, IFF, communications, electronic warfare and navigation subsystems of the surviving 381 F-111 strike/bombers in the USAF inventory

Above Tool control is strictly enforced to prevent the proverbial spanner being left in the works

Overleaf The watery light of a fine winter's morning heralds another watchful day in the life of the main control tower

RAPCON, otherwise known as the radar approach control unit, are the eyes and ears of the base. They monitor all aerial activity in the vicinity and guide the crews back home

Life at the Base

A chance for the tug to pose as the Aardvark sits on the hard stand outside its hangar

Left Summertime, and the smell of cut grass and spent jet fuel drifts across the airfield as an Aardvark performs a premeditated go-around

Above USAF Security Police ensure that only authorized personnel are allowed on the flight line, or anywhere else for that matter. There are no exceptions

Overleaf On the edge of darkness, an Aardvark departs for some serious night flying

Pages 102–103, main picture Headsets are worn by the groundcrew to speak to the pilot or WSO/EWO via the external communications cable in order to confirm preflight checks and troubleshoot any last minute hitches. **Inset, top** Detail of low-visibility 'Stars and Bars' applied to the F-111E. **Inset, bottom** Stars and stripes adorn an assortment of uniform dress

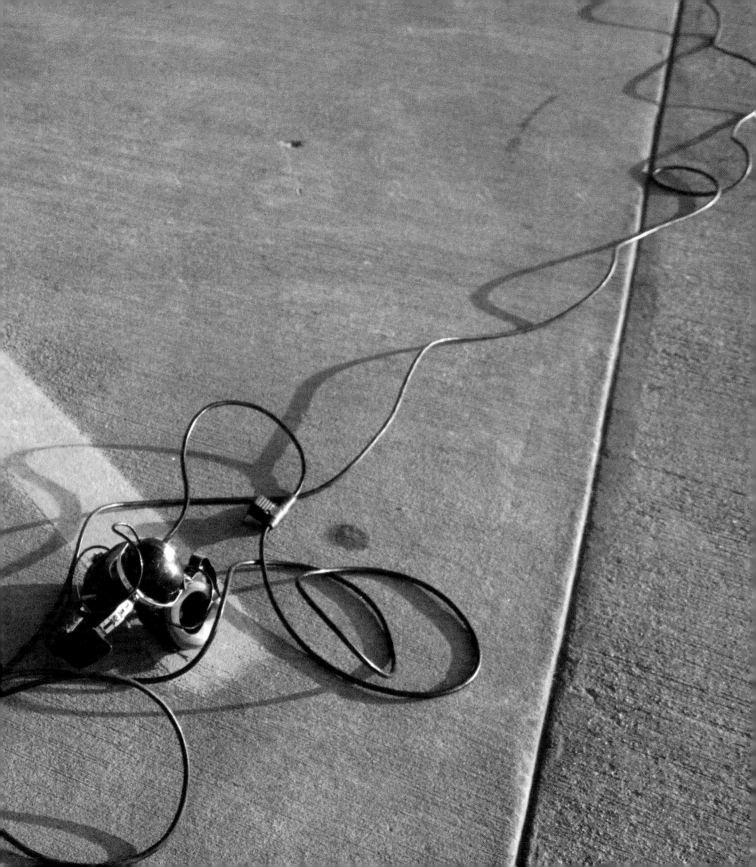

Detail of low-visibility 20th TFW insignia applied to the F-111E

Detail of 77th TFS badge applied to the nose gear door of one of their F-111Es

Right New rubber for the nose and main wheels as required

Below Close-up of the face of a TF30 engine, which features quite complex fan and compressor configurations

Right A cluster of inert Mk 82 Snakeyes: if these bombs were real the rear fins would pop out to retard them as they fell towards the target, giving the Aardvark enough time to escape the debris hemisphere of the explosions. All practice stores are painted blue

Overleaf, main picture Aircraft shelters loom on the horizon amid a sea of barley

Overleaf, inset Omnipresent USAF Security Police cruise around the perimeter watching and listening for anything out of the ordinary—such as your faithful correspondent!

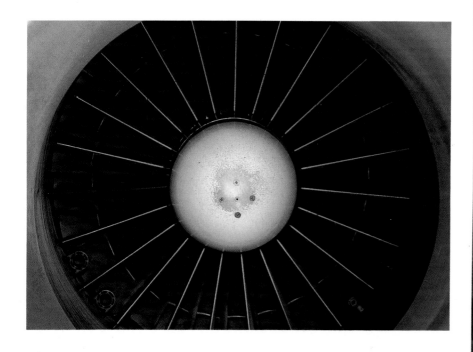

Left Two variations of the ubiquitous vans which trundle hither and thither

Above A budding recruit gets the low down on the Raven during Upper Heyford's 'Open House'

sleep tight tonight Heyford's on Alert

Right This is where the guys of the 42nd ECS relax after the day's flying is done

Above No comment!

Overleaf All of the Aardvarks at Upper Heyford are maintained in spotless condition—039 of the 77th TFS gleams in the sunshine. Despite the proximity of the inner weapons pylons to the jet intakes, interference drag does not appear to be a significant problem

Above Modellers and hobbyists who yearn for that extra little bit of detail should scrutinize this close-up of the wheel hub

Right It is 0800 Zulu: after three hours of briefing and preflight, Captain Derek Jones (pilot) and Captain Ken Williams (WSO) are about to board their mount for a 'Fini Flight' over the Luce Bay area of Scotland. Normally, this would be just another routine practice interdiction mission, but there's a surprise in store . . .

The traditional end to a last flight before being rotated back to the USA is a thorough soaking from fellow aircrew—in this case the 77th TFS. It is high noon for Captain Derek Jones (also pictured above) as he emerges from the shelter at the conclusion of his 'Fini Flight'; there is a lot of pressure in those hoses!

A distinctly damp Captain Derek Jones heads back to the 77th for a quick change of clothing before picking up his personal belongings and saying goodbye to his fellow aircrew and crew chief. His family and possessions will then travel to RAF Mildenhall (also featured in the Superbase series) for embarkation to the States

Overleaf An Aardvark heads out to the ramp, wings swept at 54 degrees for taxiing. The aircraft's 600 US gallon external fuel tanks are stored inside the shelter

Preceding pages The Raven remains in a class of its own in the West, but it is not beyond the bounds of possibility that the Soviet Union has developed an electronic warfare version of the broadly comparable Sukhoi Su-24 *Fencer*

These pages Darkness falls upon an Aardvark as its shelter beckons invitingly in the background. The bullet shaped fairing atop the vertical stabilizer (above) houses the infra-red and cryogenic line replaceable units (LRUs)

Overleaf Time for a few more go-arounds before retiring to the 42nd ECS bar